# IMPOUNDED

CIDER MILL
PRESS

BOOK
PUBLISHERS

Kennebunkport, Maine

I ♥ CROSS DRESSING

I VOTED FOR WHOEVER IS CURRENTLY SCREWING UP THE COUNTRY

# CAN'T HEAR YOU HONKING, I'M READING AN AUDIO BOOK

# IN A CAR, NO ONE CAN HEAR YOU SING

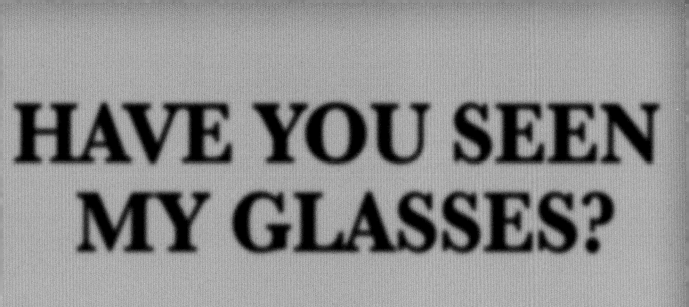

# My other bumper sticker is funny

THIS CAR IS LIKE MY HUSBAND: IT AIN'T YOURS, SO DON'T TOUCH IT!

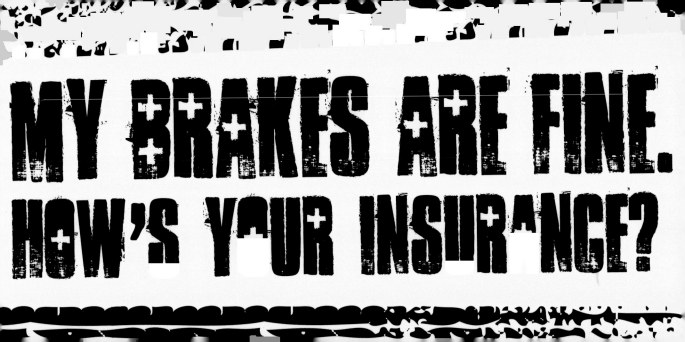

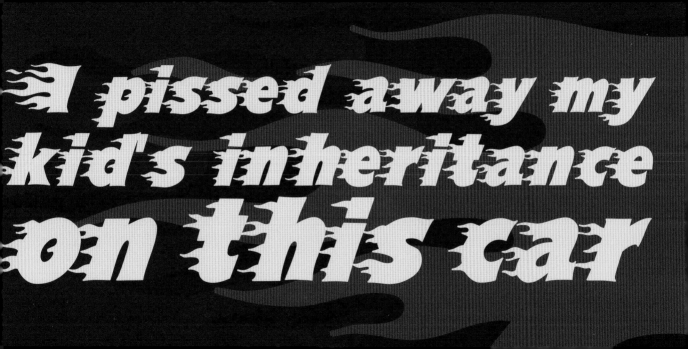

THIS TRUCK HAS BEEN IN 15 ACCIDENTS... AND IT HASN'T LOST ONE YET!

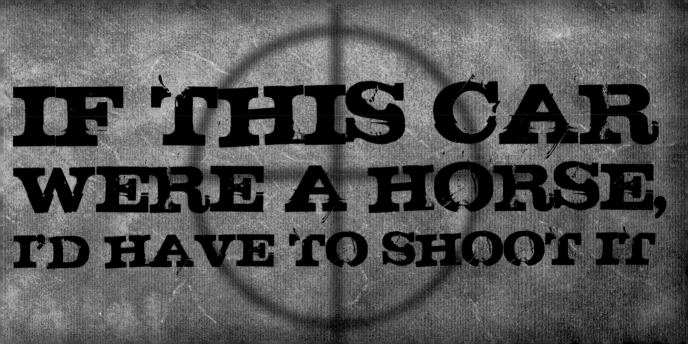

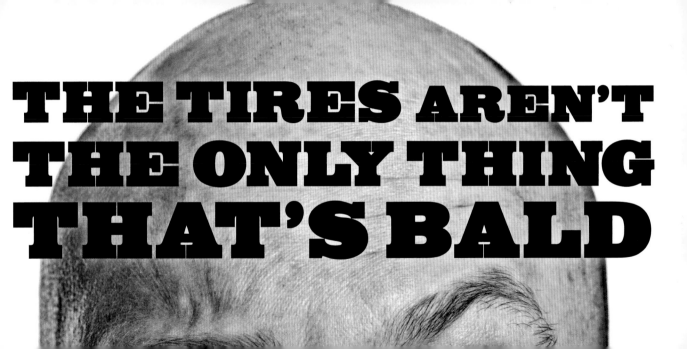

JUST DRIVING AROUND WAITING FOR AN IDIOT TO CROSS MY PATH

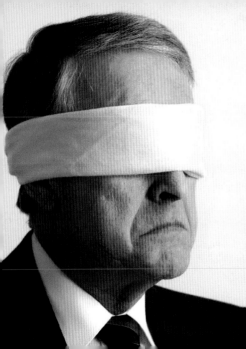

IF YOU CAN'T SEE
MY MIRRORS,
YOU'RE FREAKING
BLIND

# OBJECTS IN CAR MAY BE STUPIDER THAN THEY APPEAR

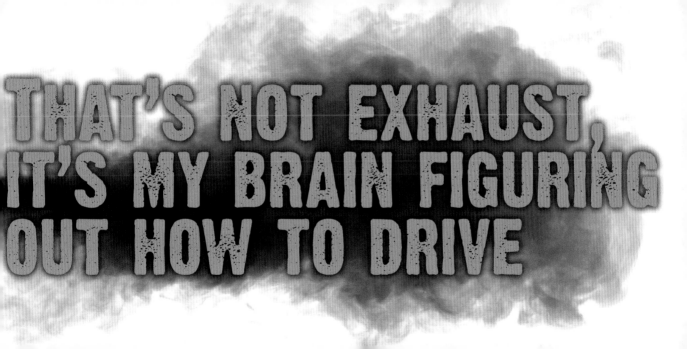

If this car is being driven courteously, it's been stolen :)

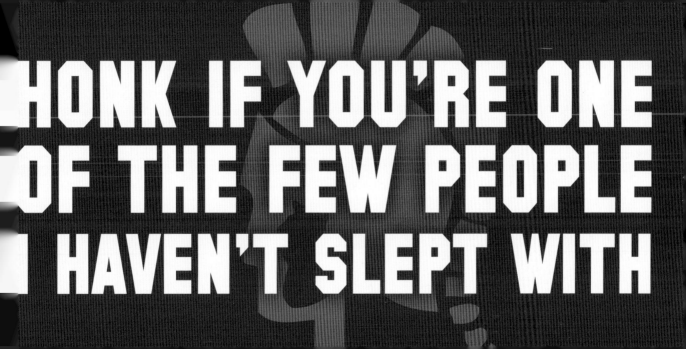

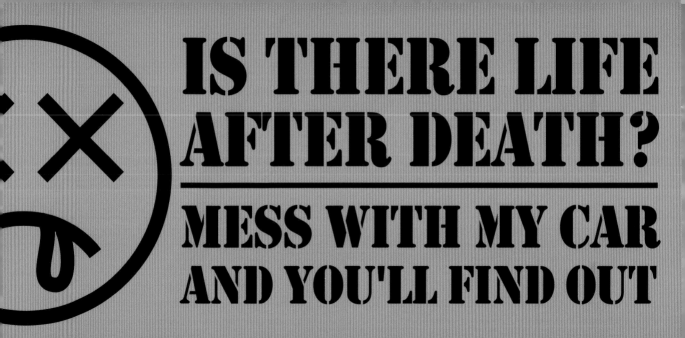

# CAR IS UNLOCKED,
# KEYS UNDER
# GERMAN SHEPHERD

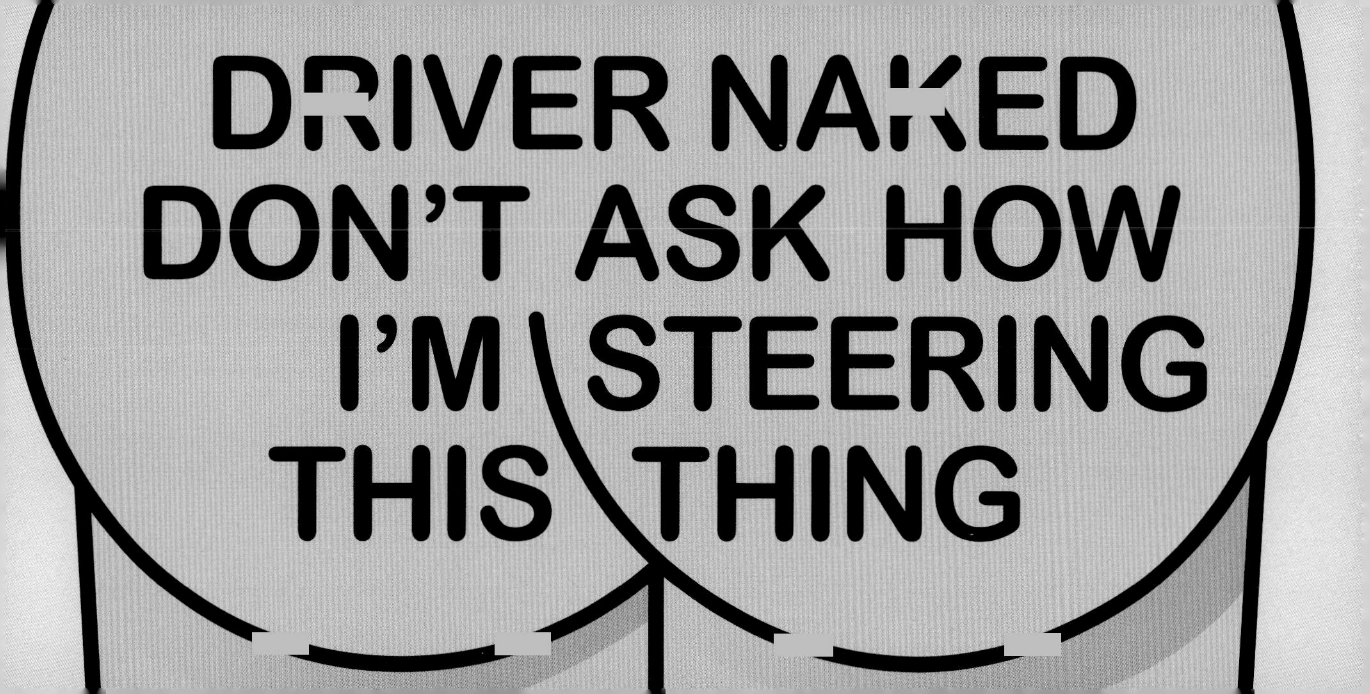
DRIVER NAKED
DON'T ASK HOW
I'M STEERING
THIS THING

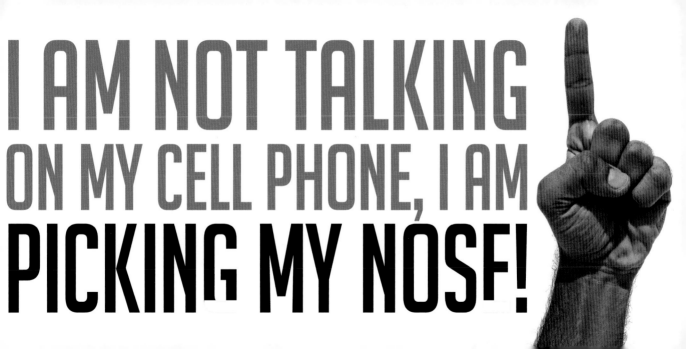

World's first
garbage can
with a steering wheel

MY OTHER CAR IS
A STRAIT JACKIT

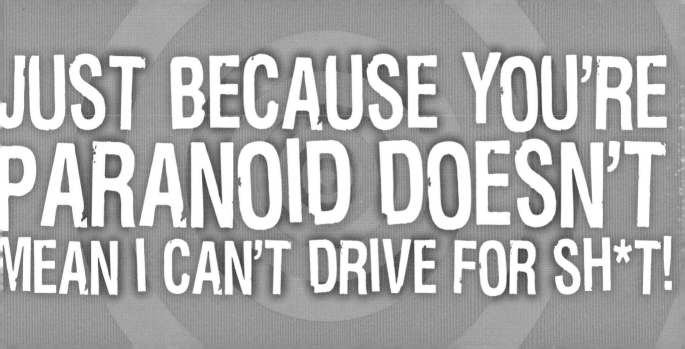

SHOPPING MALL
SMASH-UP
DERBY QUEEN

Asked the lord
for a mercedes benz,
this is all i got

# PLEASE CUSTOMIZE THIS STICKER

ASK ME ABOUT THE FINEST REST AREA MEN'S ROOMS

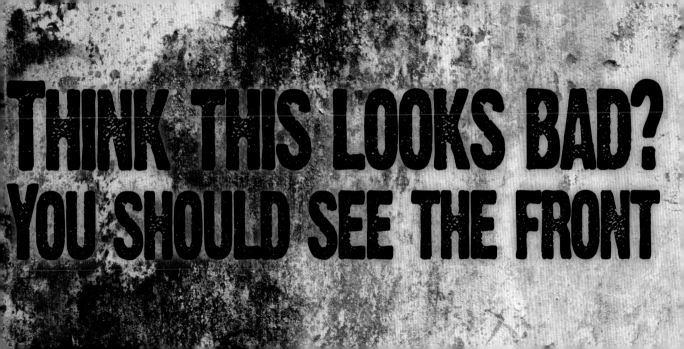

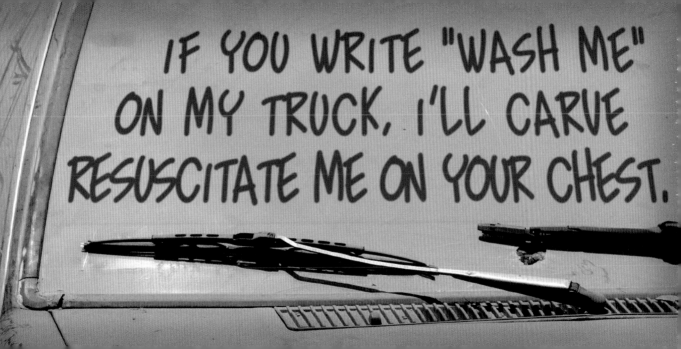

# TESTICLES OR TIRES

## THEY'RE BOTH TROUBLE

A WOMAN
AND HER TRUCK
IT'S A GREAT THING

# DRIVER OVER 70 LEFT TURN SIGNAL ON PERMANENTLY ▶

THEY COULDN'T REPAIR MY BRAKES,
SO THEY MADE MY HORN.....
# LOUDER!

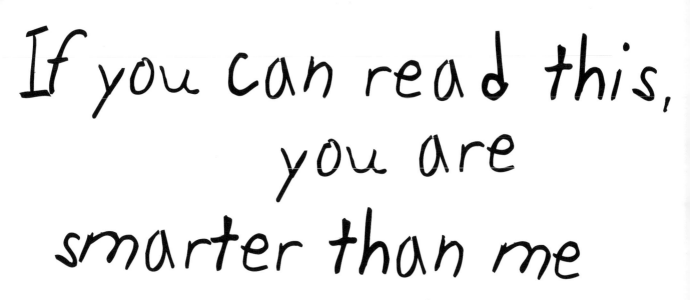

The sea and the earth are unfaithful to their children:
a truth, a faith, a generation of men goes—
and is forgotten, and it does not matter!
Except, perhaps, to the few of those
who believed the truth, confessed the faith—
or loved the men.

Joseph Conrad
*Nigger of the Narcissus*

"Sam." Elizabeth whispered his name and felt the electricity surge through her body as his mouth moved. He raised up a little so that he could look down at her. The pain and confusion were plainly written on Elizabeth's face. She spoke, but her voice was only a tiny, frail whisper. "Sam, please tell me, what's going to happen to us?"

The question pierced through him again and again. He had asked himself that many times, but to hear it on her lips gave it a power he didn't want to acknowledge. Sam stared at her eyes, and then her mouth, and with great effort the answer finally came from his lips. "I wish I knew, Elizabeth. I wish to God I knew. . . ."

Andrea Davidson was born in Oklahoma and attended the University of Missouri. She began her writing career with the American Medical Association, and after the birth of her first child she became a free-lance writer for magazines and medical journals, as well as a free-lance editor for several Chicago publishers.

After moving to Houston, Texas, where she now resides with her husband and family, Andrea started her romance-writing career.

THE GOLDEN CAGE is Andrea Davidson's first novel for WORLDWIDE.

# THE
# GOLDEN
# CAGE

BY

ANDREA DAVIDSON

**WORLDWIDE ROMANCE**

London ● Sydney ● Toronto

*First published in Great Britain in 1986
by Worldwide Romance
15–16 Brook's Mews, London W1A 1DR*

*This Paperback edition published in 1987
by Worldwide Romance*

*Australian copyright 1984
Philippine copyright 1984*

© Susan L. Lowe 1984

ISBN 0 373 50388 1

The quote from NIGGER OF THE NARCISSUS by Joseph Conrad is by kind permission of the Trustees of the Joseph Conrad Estate.

09–0487

*Printed and bound in Great Britain by
Cox & Wyman Ltd, Reading*

## Chapter One

The shrill screech of metal wheels against metal track pierced the stagnant air with ruthless intensity as the elevated train rounded the curve on its route into downtown Chicago. Below the track on Blackhawk Street, in the tired, run-down area near the Turning Basin, a ceiling of brown hung like a heavy tarp over the late morning, a dull half-light that clung in brooding shadows to the withered facades of old buildings. Superfluous human forms loitered, aimless and apathetic, between the paint-chipped frames of doorways. All were indifferent to the passing commuter train.

Harry Finklemann, the pug-faced owner and operator of The Windy City Pawn Shop, was too busy bilking people out of their most treasured possessions to notice. If a sheep had fleece, it was a sure bet slippery Harry would find a way to shear it, and that was all that concerned him on this cool October morning.

Alvaro Eugenio-Montes-Ciruti Rodriguez, on the other hand, was too drunk to acknowledge much of anything. He was leaning against the side wall of the liquor store, his brown felt hat pulled down so low, it pushed his ears straight out to the sides like flaps. The neck of a bottle of Thunderbird protruded from the brown paper sack in his hand, and a silly grin plastered itself across his face.

Across the street, Maggie Moon was busy searching for treasures. Mumbling aloud to herself, she bent over and picked up an abandoned brown left boot, examining it closely. She stood it next to her own left foot and decided it would do quite nicely. Arguing loudly with herself on whether to house it in her green shopping bag or in her purple, she finally decided on the purple, then shuffled on down the street, rounding the corner where two skinny teen-agers huddled together and exchanged a thick wad of bills for a tiny packet of fine white powder.

None of them paid any attention to the train screaming along the tracks above them. Only Sam Winslow observed it, and he was trying to suppress a twinge of corrosive resentment for the apathy that was aboard the train.

He was walking down the sidewalk on his way to the Blackhawk mission as the train passed. Neighbors, leaning over the pigeon-mottled sills of second floor windows, greeted him with a smile and the dust from their flapping rugs. Those on the sidewalk nodded as they swept away the nightly accumulation of debris in front of their wilting shops.

Everyone on Blackhawk Street knew Sam Winslow.

He had a muscular build, an easy gait, a sturdy, handsome quality about him. His sandy-brown hair was carelessly groomed, his corduroy jeans faded, and his tan poplin jacket sported a couple of unfashionable iron-on patches. But it was his eyes that were most often remembered. A soft autumn brown, they radiated both self-confidence and an optimism rarely seen in this part of the city.

Although at this moment the optimism was hidden behind his annoyance as he stared up at the train. All eyes behind its windows were buried in the newspaper headlines, sheltered from the harshness of life below the tracks, divorced from its grim reality. Not one face had turned to the windows to take note of the disintegrating neighborhood below. Not one.

He knew that within minutes the train would ease into the downtown Loop, where the city crackled with the electricity of life and prosperity. There, newspapers would be folded and slipped into briefcases and the passengers would emerge from their iron-gray cocoon, safe at last from the threatening world only two miles to the northwest.

Sam took a shortcut across a vacant lot, but he stopped when he saw three young boys clamber up the tall steel supports to the tracks. A sense of panic began to rise within him as a vision of the tiny lifeless body he helped carry down from the tracks only a month ago flashed across his mind's eye.

He ran toward the boys, trying to catch them before they reached the top, but they were too far ahead of him. He yelled, but his warning was lost in the deafening clamor of wheels rattling against the metal rail.

Now in position, holding tight to the top of the iron posts, they hurled empty bottles at the train and hollered with delight at the sound of splintering glass. Then quickly they scrambled back down the supports, shrieking deliriously at their own bravado.

Sam caught up with them as they reached the bottom. He grabbed one of the boy's arms, but the other two got away. His heart was pounding with the memory of the little boy who had not been so lucky a month ago, and it filled him with impotent fury.

His eyes wide with mutinous protest, the captured boy stared at him, daring Sam to make the first move. The deadlock lasted only a moment before Sam loosened his hold and dropped his hands to his side. For a second the boy stood still and then, with a triumphant laugh, disappeared behind a rusty heap of abandoned cars and battered washing machines.

Sam let out a slow breath and shook his head in frustration. Here, every day was an uphill climb, but surely he would eventually reach some plateau where life would level off and become a little easier. He knew he had made some progress in this neighborhood since he came here a few years ago; but he also knew he still had a hell of a long way to go.

He lifted his eyes toward the tracks. The fading squall of the train as it hurried on its journey to downtown was like the cry of a child, carried on the wind in a long, lost sob.

Elizabeth drew open the heavy drapes with a flourish and clasped her hands together in anticipation of the response. To the delight of her guests, the strategically lighted lawn with its kidney-shaped pool and brick patio was revealed in all its splendor. The new waterfall had finally been completed and everyone at the party was just dying to see it.

Amidst the expected "ooohs" and "aahhs," Elizabeth mingled like the perfect hostess she was, shimmering blond hair swinging across her shoulders as she laughed gaily at one of the guest's not-so-witty remarks, and long emerald-green silk skirt swishing as she moved gracefully through the crowd.

If a prize were given to the loveliest hostess on Chicago's North Shore, it would surely have gone to Elizabeth Parkins. She was tall and willowy, with a pale softness that triggered a soaring pulse in any man around her.

The men adored her. The women envied her. And everyone fell all over themselves in attempts to be noticed by her. She was indeed a lucky woman.

Elizabeth yawned, then quickly scanned the room, hoping no one had observed the breach of etiquette. It was the typical crowd in their latest Paris creations. The same old stories, the same old faces. The same old sameness. She raised her glass to one of the handsome men across the room, and the playful smile she flashed at him could have dazzled the heavens.

Despite the indistinct tuggings of boredom, the sounds of the party were reassuring ones to her, familiar and reliable—the clinking of fine-cut crystal, the sonorous drone of inane small talk, even the low hum of careless elitist remarks. "Of course, my dear," she heard a woman say. "Our organization has donated a small fortune to those poor little colored people over there in the Sudan." The woman was rewarded with one of Elizabeth's prettiest smiles as she walked by.

Platters heaped with untouched but now tepid delicacies were carried by the help to the kitchen, where their contents were dumped unceremoniously down the disposal. Every now and then one of the maids with the catering service would dip a tiny shrimp in its sauce or spread a wafer with pâté before it was thrown away, but even they had grown used to excess and its tendency toward extravagant waste.

Adrienne Stebbins walked over to Elizabeth and studied her hostess and best friend with a mixture of admiration and jealousy. "Liz darling, you've been holding out on me. Wherever did you get that divine dress?"

"I had it made." Elizabeth smiled. "Do you really like it?"

"I love it."

"You look lovely too, Adrienne."

Adrienne picked at her dress. "Hmmm, thanks." She laughed. "God, would you listen to us. We sound like the mutual admiration society. But speaking of dressmakers, do you remember Janette Brenner? Don't you remember, she was at Vassar with us and she was studying to become a designer?"

Elizabeth laughed as the recollection came back to her. "Oh, sure. How could I forget her? She was the one who always had fifty pins stuck in her mouth and bolts of cloth following her down the hallways. Did she make it?"

"Amazingly enough, yes," Adrienne answered smugly. "And she's going to be here next month, showing at Saks. Let's go see what kind of rags she is designing, want to?"

"I'd love to. It sounds like fun."

"And don't forget that project on the west side you volunteered us for."

"What project?" Elizabeth asked.

"Uh-oh," Adrienne groaned, "here comes Melanie Hearndon. I don't think I can handle a conversation with her right now. We'll talk later," she whispered conspiratorially.

Elizabeth watched Melanie moving toward her, so she readied her smile. "Melanie dear, so glad you could make it."

"Liz, you always throw such marvelous parties. Have you met my cousin, Thomas Benson?" The auburn-haired woman linked her arm through the man's as she introduced him to her hostess.

Elizabeth held out a jeweled hand, and he lifted it to his lips, his eyes locking with hers for a glittering moment. He was quite handsome, elegant one would say, with almost-black hair that was styled to perfection. And those blue eyes! The way they followed her curves as if he would devour her.

She had heard all about Thomas Benson. In fact, she had heard of almost nothing else since he had come to town. Extraordinarily wealthy, dashing, debonair, and on and on and on. She had been positive that the man would turn out to be a terrible disappointment in person. However. . . maybe she should ask him to stay for a drink after the party.

Her sweeping glance took in the other men at the party. Since none of those in her social circle needed to work, very few of them did. Mostly they just hung around the club every day, riding horses as a prelude to rounds of drinks—that being the main event of the day—playing cards as an adjunct to rounds of drinks, and attempting halfhearted business deals as a finale to too many rounds of drinks.

The image made her uncommonly weary.

She slipped her hand from Thomas Benson's grasp, dodging with perfect ease any implied invitation his eyes might have held. "So glad you could make it tonight. I do hope you will be able to come with Melanie to my dinner party next Friday."

"If I'm still in town, I would love to come," he replied with just the right touch of aplomb.

Relieved that the more amorous moment had passed, she turned toward her other guests, her smile generous and irresistible. But the smile faded when she was faced with the disapproving frown of her mother, Louise Parkins Banning—Banning being the latest in a long line of husbands.

"He appeared to be a charming young man, Liz. Who was he?"

"I don't know. Benson something or other."

"Really, dear, you must try to remember names better. It's a reflection of your breeding, you know." Louise sloshed her drink over the rim of her glass. "Ooops."

Elizabeth's smile was restrained. "Yes, Mother, breeding."

Her mother, as well as all of her friends, were always pushing one eligible bachelor after another at her. They simply could not get it through their heads that she had no desire to marry. "Liz, you're thirty years old," her mother would whisper in incriminatingly hushed tones, relegating her daughter to the status of one who has some unmentionable social disease.

It was true that she was a curiosity among her set. Though there were other single men and women around, they were most often the products of divorce. None of them had never been married! Why, it was unheard of. That sort of thing was supposed to be reserved for feminists, gays, or—worse yet—working women.

But, then, perhaps it was her single status that enhanced the intriguing aura around Elizabeth. After all, it gave the men someone about whom to fantasize, and it gave the women someone to secretly pick to pieces.

Louise pursed her lips. "You're frowning, Liz. I hope that doesn't mean you're getting petulant. It does not become you, love. Did I remind you about the committee that's being set up? No, I didn't, did I? The members of the Guild are expecting you to head up their new fund-raising drive, so you mustn't disappoint them."

Elizabeth reached out to steady her mother's glass, but Louise continued without missing a beat. "You have such a flair for those types of things. Besides, you know how important this fund-raising is to your grandmother, not to mention what it will do to enhance your own standing. Liz, are you listening to me?"

Elizabeth's bright green eyes were scanning the room, making sure with inbred efficiency that each of her guest's needs were being assuaged. But she forced her attention to swing back to her mother. "I'm listening, I'm listening."

"Well, will you do it?"

"Yes, Mother, of course." Her tone was that of the dutiful daughter she had been taught to be.

"Good." The older woman nodded in satisfaction, grabbing her sixth glass of champagne off a passing tray. "And don't forget, on Wednesday your grandmother is giving her report at the Book Review Club and

she expects you to be there. She says this book is *the* definitive work on societal decline in this country. You will be there?''

''Wouldn't miss it for the world,'' Elizabeth mumbled dryly. ''Oh, Joan!'' She waved to a woman she absolutely abhorred. ''Sorry, Mother, but I've been dying to hear about Joan's trip to Spain.''

''Well, all right,'' Louise said. ''Do you want me to stay after the party to help clean up? You know how these hired maids are. They never put anything where it belongs.''

Elizabeth watched her mother closely. Louise's expression was as sober as a judge, but she held her glass at a sharp angle and a steady trickle of champagne poured to the carpet.

''No, thank you, Mother. I can handle it.'' Elizabeth sighed and turned toward her guests. She lifted her shoulders, adjusted her smile, and moved through the crowd with grace and beauty, the regal princess at home among her adoring subjects.

Mama Vinzetti handed Sam another dish to dry. ''Sam, it's nearly seven o'clock. You've done more than enough. Why don't you go on home.''

''I'll help you finish up here. There certainly was a crowd out there today.''

Mama Vinzetti plunged her hands into the hot soapy water. ''Lots of hungry people.''

The mission's staff of eager volunteers was irregular—their rotation determined by the lunar cycle or perhaps only by whims of conscience. For whatever reason, the soup kitchen was often shorthanded, and when it was, Sam pitched in.

He stacked the unmatched plates and bowls in the cupboard above the sink and wiped a few beads of sweat from his forehead with the sleeve of his plaid shirt.

Though the stove had been turned off for some time, the heat from it was still almost overwhelming.

"Come on now, Sam, you've done enough. I've got Anna here with me, and you know how good she is in a kitchen." She turned a sly eye on him. "Maybe she will come cook for you someday, yes?"

Sam cleared his throat and looked away, but he found himself staring straight into the hot, hungry stare of Anna Vinzetti.

From Chicago Avenue to North Avenue and from Ashland to Halsted, everyone knew of Mama Vinzetti's crusade in life. She carried it out with the inexhaustible vitality of her Italian heritage and with the dogged perseverance of a zealous crusader in a savage land. Her well-intentioned campaign? To find a man for her nineteen-year-old daughter, Anna.

This might not have been such a difficult task, except for the fact that Anna was five feet eleven inches tall, weighed two hundred pounds, and had a sexual appetite that could debilitate the entire infield of the Chicago White Sox.

And Sam, being no fool, was fully aware that he was the latest target for which Mama Vinzetti and Anna's passionate cupid bow was aimed.

Swallowing certain emasculating feelings of being outweighed and outnumbered by these two very determined, confident women, Sam grabbed his jacket from the back of a chair and stepped out the door.

"See you tomorrow, Sam." Anna's low slur stroked the back of his neck, sending unwanted prickles all the way down his spine.

"Sure, Anna. Sure." He shoved his hands into the pockets of his jacket and hurried out into the evening.

From his pocket he extracted an apple he had tucked away and raised it to his mouth. But before he could

take the first bite, his eyes landed on Billy Hawkins, better known on the street as "The Mole."

The grizzled, arthritic old man, who always wore the same long, tattered brown coat, was, with single-minded determination, rummaging through an over-flowing trash can.

After finding a discarded can of red beans, Billy scraped the remains with his finger and poked it in his mouth. He smiled broadly, his unshaven face framing a toothless grin, as Sam walked up to him.

"Come with me, Billy," he said. "Let's go get something to eat." As expected, Billy shook his head vehemently, his eyes darting about in agitation, and Sam tried to hide his impatience with the old man. Billy had his ways, just as the street did, and nothing or nobody was going to change them.

Sam thought of some of the arguments he had used in the past, but decided against all of them. Instead, he offered the apple. Without a moment's hesitation Billy nodded his thanks and greedily accepted it, then dropped down to the sidewalk and beat the fruit against the pavement, splitting and smashing it into manageable bites.

He looked up, grinning, and Sam smiled. "You're welcome, Billy." A few harrowed lines appeared at the corner of Sam's mouth as he moved on down the side-walk toward home.

He walked up the precarious stoop of his Victorian house, sidestepping the wood rot and loose boards on the steps. There were lots of things he would like to do to fix up the old house, but those things took time and money, two commodities he didn't have right now.

Sam unlocked the front door and noticed that the crack in its beveled glass pane had lengthened at least half an inch since last week.

Once inside, he emptied the pockets of his jacket and

tossed his keys and several scraps of paper onto the table by the coat rack. He unfolded one of the pieces of paper and frowned as he tried to decipher his own handwriting. Elizabeth Parkins, it said. Who was she and why had he written down her name?

He was always jotting reminders to himself and then stuffing them into pockets where he promptly forgot all about them. But he did recall now that he had written down this name several days ago. Elizabeth Parkins was the chairman of a select coterie of wealthy North Shore socialites who had volunteered to come look over the hospital tomorrow.

Sam wadded up the piece of paper and tossed it back onto the table. He had seen too many of these self-proclaimed philanthropists come and go in the last five years to get his hopes up with this group.

He hung his jacket on the coat rack, then grabbed his White Sox baseball cap off a hook and put it on. He flipped on the radio to the Monday night football game and stared into the near-empty refrigerator. He had forgotten, as usual, to stop at the market, so he was short on food as well as everything else. But, nothing new about that.

He ended up with a grilled cheese sandwich and a soda while he listened for the score of the game. One of these days he was going to scrape up enough money to go to Soldier Field and watch the Bears play. Someday.

He switched stations on the radio when he heard how bad his team was playing and tuned in some classical music. After cleaning up his dishes, he poured a glass of wine, carried it into the small living room, and set it on a lopsided table by the faded, overstuffed chair where he sat each night to read.

He crossed the room to the window and looked out, watching the night emerge. The street imparted a different texture after the sun went down, a frenetic, almost desperate energy of lonely people playing the only roles they knew. He rested his knuckles on the windowsill as he watched the electricity charge the night.

His thoughts filtered back to a night fourteen years ago, when he stood at the window in his fraternity house, much as he was now with his hands resting on the sill. Another form of reckless energy galvanized the air as the Chi O's invaded the Kappa Alpha house next door. It was a reverse panty raid, an oddity in itself, but especially so in those troubled days of rage.

That morning, word was out that United States and South Vietnamese troops had invaded Cambodia. The demonstrations on the Wisconsin campus had been particularly riotous and bitter all day, with overwrought students responding to rabid leaders of the Students for a Democratic Society. It had seemed to Sam on that day that the world had come unhinged. Nothing was as it should be; maybe nothing ever would be again. And, in the midst of all of this, here were these fair-haired girls from the Chi Omega house, with their creamy thighs and uptight virtue, out on the lawn in their short nightgowns, expending their own form of mindless energy.

Funny that he should think of that night now, that inadvertent turning point in his life. It had all happened so long ago.

He moved away from the window. There were thin cotton chintz curtains hanging there, but he didn't bother to close them. Life on the street was a part of him and he a part of it, so it had never seemed necessary to shut himself off from it. This was where he lived.

He sat down in his old chair and picked up *The Fratricides* by Nikos Kazantzakis. On the radio Mozart's Concerto in F Major was playing. He opened the novel and continued reading. As was often the case, Sam was alone. He would prefer that it not be so, but it was okay. He was a man who had given up expecting a lot out of life, so he was rarely disappointed.

And tomorrow would just be another day. He would probably help out at the mission again. He needed to find a building to hold the counseling sessions for juvenile parolees. That committee of North Shore debutantes would come to the hospital and might or might not decide to donate time or money. Just another day.

In the yellow glow of the lamp he read. And the window lay bare to the cool October night on Blackhawk Street.


The party was over, the guests had departed, and Elizabeth deflated. Like a punctured plastic blow-up doll, she lost her air. Her smiling exterior caved in upon her, stifling, squeezing.

It wasn't the first time she had experienced the feeling. But she had no idea what to do about it. Maybe her mother was right. Maybe she should get married. At least then she wouldn't have to face the long nights alone.

It was so quiet in the house, except for the soft chatter of the maids as they emptied ashtrays and carried glasses and plates to the kitchen to be washed.

Elizabeth walked to the bare window and stared out into the dark at the flawlessly manicured back lawn. Tomorrow a crew was supposed to come and empty the pool to ready it for winter. She opened the French doors and listened to the waterfall as it trickled and gurgled over the skillfully aligned rocks. It had impressed her guests as she had anticipated. But now the sound that reached her ears was lonely in its repetitiveness. Lonely and sad.

She closed the door and latched it tightly, wondering with a bubble of apprehension if perhaps she should have asked Thomas Benson to stay. At least it would have been company, someone with whom to talk, perhaps even to hold through the night.

She shrugged, picked up a pillow from the couch, and then distractedly tossed it back. But then, what could they possibly have talked about that would have been new and different?

And as for anything more intimate, it was far too much trouble anyway. She would have had to be charming and sexy. He probably would have expected champagne tonight and breakfast in bed tomorrow.

Too much trouble.

Wouldn't it be nice if she could wake up in the morning to some new and wondrous adventure? Her bitter laugh followed the weak moment of irrational fantasy. No, tomorrow would bring nothing more exciting than a few tennis tips from that handsome new pro at the club.

A wave of fatigue swept over her. She turned to her maid, who was cleaning away the debris. "Letti," she said, "let the caterers out when they're finished and turn out the lights, will you?"

"Yes, Miss Elizabeth."

Closing the heavy drapes to shut out the dark, lonely night, Elizabeth walked through the living room to the foyer and slowly climbed the sweeping staircase, following the gilded hallway to the white frills and flounces of her exquisitely furnished bedroom.

# *Chapter Two*

"Would you please stop shouting, Adrienne! For God's sake, I have the phone a foot from my ear and I can still hear you bellowing."

"If you were here, Liz, I wouldn't be yelling."

"Where?" Elizabeth frowned. "You sound so far away."

"I am far away," Adrienne hissed through the wires. "About as far away from civilization as you can get. The question is, why the hell aren't you here too?"

Elizabeth sighed and glanced over at the peach tennis outfit lying on her bed. Five more minutes and she would have been out of here. She just hated that puffed-up drawl Adrienne used when she was in one of her little snits.

"Start at the beginning." She plopped down on the edge of her bed and waited for the explanation.

"I'm talking about this west side hospital thing you roped me into. Dammit, Liz, you're chairwoman of this stupid committee. Why I ever volunteered to help out with this..."

Elizabeth blanched. "It's today!" She frantically started flipping through her date book on the bedside table, searching for the reminder. "Oh, damn, I forgot to write it down. I had forgotten all about it."

"Well, it is today," Adrienne snipped. "And I for